DINOSAUR WARS

SPINOSAURUS

★★★★★★★★★★

VS

GIGANOTOSAURUS

★★★★★★★★★★

BATTLE OF THE GIANTS

Michael O'Hearn

Consultant:
Mathew J. Wedel, PhD
Paleontologist

Raintree

www.raintreepublishers.co.uk
Visit our website to find out
more information about
Raintree books.

To order:
☎ Phone 0845 6044371
📄 Fax +44 (0) 1865 312263
✉ Email myorders@raintreepublishers.co.uk

Customers from outside the UK please telephone +44 1865 312262

Raintree is an imprint of Capstone Global Library Limited, a company incorporated
in England and Wales having its registered office at 7 Pilgrim Street, London,
EC4V 6LB – Registered company number: 6695582

Text © Capstone Press 2010
First published in hardback in the United Kingdom by Capstone Global Library in 2011
The moral rights of the proprietor have been asserted.

Editors: Aaron Sautter and Laura Knowles
Designer: Kyle Grenz
Media Researcher: Marcie Spence
Art Director: Nathan Gassman
Production Specialist: Laura Manthe
Illustrations by Philip Renne, Jon Hughes, and James Field
Originated by Capstone Global Library Ltd
Printed and bound in China by South China Printing Company Ltd

ISBN 978 1 406 21819 0 (hardback)
14 13 12 11 10
10 9 8 7 6 5 4 3 2 1

British Library Cataloguing in Publication Data
A full catalogue record for this book is available from the British Library.

Acknowledgements
We would like to thank the following for permission to reproduce photographs: Brett Booth
pp. **6 left**, **18–19 bottom**; Photo Researchers, Inc **cover top** (Joe Tucciarone/Science Photo
Library); Shutterstock **parchment backgrounds** (Valery Potapova), **stylized backgrounds**
(Leigh Prather).

Disclaimer
All the Internet addresses (URLs) given in this book were valid at the time of going to press.
However, due to the dynamic nature of the Internet, some addresses may have changed, or
sites may have changed or ceased to exist since publication. While the author and Publishers
regret any inconvenience this may cause readers, no responsibility for any such changes can
be accepted by either the author or the publisher.

CONTENTS

WELCOME TO DINOSAUR WARS! 4

THE COMBATANTS 6

SIZE 8

SPEED AND AGILITY 10

WEAPONS 12

ATTACK STYLE 16

GET READY TO RUMBLE! 18

THE BATTLE 20

GLOSSARY 30

FIND OUT MORE 31

INDEX 32

WELCOME TO DINOSAUR WARS!

Dinosaurs were brutal creatures. They fought each other and ate each other. Usually it was meat-eater versus plant-eater or big versus small. But in Dinosaur Wars, it's a free for all. Plant-eaters attack plant-eaters. Giants fight giants. And small dinosaurs gang up on huge opponents. In Dinosaur Wars, any dinosaur battle is possible!

In this dinosaur war, Spinosaurus and Giganotosaurus battle to the death. You will see how these massive meat-eaters match up. You'll learn about their giant weapons and how they used them in combat. Then you'll see them battling head-to-head – and you'll get to watch from a front row seat!

Spinosaurus (SPINE-oh-sore-us)
Giganotosaurus (gig-an-OH-toe-sore-us)

THE COMBATANTS

SPINOSAURUS VS GIGANOTOSAURUS

Spinosaurus and Giganotosaurus never actually fought. Spinosaurus lived on the northern coast of Africa. Meanwhile, Giganotosaurus lived at the southern tip of South America.

Still, before they became **extinct**, they did share the earth for 5 million years. Giganotosaurus survived for 22 million years, from about 112 to 90 million years ago. Spinosaurus lived from about 95 to 70 million years ago.

These were two of the largest **predators** ever to walk the earth. They probably wouldn't have hunted each other. However, if they had lived in the same area, they may have fought over a meal. After all, they were both so big that they had to eat a lot of food.

Tyrannosaurus rex was once thought to be the largest land predator ever. But both Spinosaurus and Giganotosaurus were longer and heavier than T. rex. They are the largest known land predators of all time.

FIERCE FACT

BIGGEST PREDATORS

extinct no longer living anywhere in the world

predator animal that hunts other animals for food

SIZE

Spinosaurus
18 metres long; 8.2 tonnes
★ ★ ★ ★ ★

★ ★ ★ ★ ★
Giganotosaurus
12 metres long; 7.7 tonnes

Spinosaurus was up to 18 metres (59 feet) long from head to tail. That's about the same length as a bendy bus. Spinosaurus' head measured almost 1.8 metres (6 feet) long. He had a spiny sail on his back, similar to the back fins of many fish. The sail stood more than 1.8 metres (6 feet) high at the tallest point. Spinosaurus weighed more than 8.2 tonnes. He had the size and strength to overpower almost anything that got in his way.

Giganotosaurus was one of the few creatures in history that could match Spinosaurus in size. At around 12 metres (39 feet) long, Giganotosaurus was shorter than Spinosaurus. But what Giganotosaurus lacked in length, he made up for in weight. He tipped the scales at about 7.7 tonnes. Although he was slightly smaller than Spinosaurus, Giganotosaurus would still be tough to beat in a fight.

SPEED AND AGILITY

Spinosaurus
Sleek and quick
★ ★ ★

★ ★
Giganotosaurus
Stocky and powerful

Giganotosaurus had strong back legs and probably ran fast for short distances. But with his stockier frame, it is unlikely he could stop or turn quickly. Giganotosaurus probably hunted giant long-necked dinosaurs that didn't move quickly. He didn't need to be fast to be a successful hunter.

Spinosaurus was sleeker and more streamlined than the stocky Giganotosaurus. He could probably move quickly on land. But Spinosaurus had a bigger advantage in the water, where he hunted for most of his food. With his streamlined body, he could wade into deep water and still move quickly. Spinosaurus' quickness would be a big advantage in a fight.

SPINOSAURUS' WEAPONS

Spinosaurus had a long, flat snout like a crocodile. His long jaws were full of huge, deadly teeth. But unlike most **carnivores**, Spinosaurus had teeth that were spaced fairly far apart. They were straight, smooth, and cone-shaped. They were made for stabbing through meat rather than slicing it. Scientists think his teeth and jaws were made for catching fish instead of killing large **prey** on land.

FIERCE FACT
DESTROYED FOSSILS

The first Spinosaurus fossils ever discovered were destroyed in a bombing raid in Germany during World War II (1939–1945). No other Spinosaurus fossils were found until the 1980s.

Like many other predators, Spinosaurus had three clawed fingers on each hand. But while many large meat-eaters had very short arms, Spinosaurus' arms were much longer. Being able to reach further may have given him an advantage against Giganotosaurus.

carnivore animal that eats only meat
prey animal that is hunted by other animals

GIGANOTOSAURUS' WEAPONS

At 20 centimetres (8 inches) long, Giganotosaurus' teeth were enormous. They were flat like a shark's teeth, but they were longer and narrower. They were **serrated** like a knife blade to slice through flesh and cause a lot of bleeding.

If Giganotosaurus got hold of his enemies, they were in trouble. Although he was a little smaller than Spinosaurus, his jaws were much more powerful. His superior bite strength would be a huge advantage in any fight.

serrated having a jagged edge

The first Giganotosaurus skeleton was discovered in Argentina by a car mechanic who hunted for fossils in his spare time.

FIERCE FACT

FOSSILS

Giganotosaurus also had sharp claws on each of his six fingers. He could use these curved claws for slashing an enemy or gripping his prey.

ATTACK STYLE

Spinosaurus was built to hunt in the water and on land. Evidence shows that he ate fish and other dinosaurs. His long snout and unique teeth were made to grab and hang on to wildly squirming prey. With his long arms, he could stab at fish in the water or grab a victim on land. His neck was longer than the necks of most large meat-eaters. It allowed him to quickly dart his head forward to grab prey. In a fight, his long neck would provide a reach advantage against Giganotosaurus.

Spinosaurus' nostrils sat fairly high up on his snout. This feature allowed him to keep part of his snout underwater while still breathing.

Some scientists think Giganotosaurus hunted in packs. It might seem unnecessary for such a large predator, but hunting in packs would have helped bring down huge prey. Giganotosaurus probably hunted mighty **herbivores** like Argentinosaurus, which weighed about 90 tonnes. A pack of Giganotosaurus probably bit their prey again and again. Each bite would tear away chunks of flesh until the victim bled to death.

GET READY TO RUMBLE!

Are you ready for the main event? Two giant meat-eaters are out to prove who's the biggest, most dangerous beast of the prehistoric world. In one corner is the fierce hunter – Spinosaurus! He's big, he's tough, and he's mean. In the other corner is his opponent – Giganotosaurus! His name says it all. He's gigantic, deadly, and hungry. Nobody can guess which of these super-sized dinosaurs will win this fight. But one thing is certain – the winner will be bloody, battered, and bruised!

You've got a front row seat. So sit back, turn the page, and get ready to enjoy the battle!

SPINOSAURUS

★ ★ ★ ★ ★ SIZE

SPEED AND AGILITY ★ ★ ★ ★ ★

WEAPONS ★ ★ ★ ★ ★

ATTACK STYLE ★ ★ ★ ★ ★ ★

GIGANOTOSAURUS

ONE LAST THING...

This battle is make-believe. Like Goldilocks and the three bears – it never happened. Even scientists don't know everything about these two mighty dinosaurs. But we do know they were big, mean, and hungry – and they could fight. This should be one gigantic good show!

THE BATTLE

Spinosaurus splashes through the ocean. He cranes his neck low and scans the water. Just beyond him, stormy waves crash down. Foamy water rumbles towards the shore. Neither the rain nor the violent sea seems to bother the monstrous Spinosaurus.

Suddenly, he plunges his long snout into the salty water. His jaws snap shut. Below the surface, his teeth bite into the tail of a long, brown fish. He jerks his snout upward to pull the fish from the water. The fish thrashes wildly and begins to slip from his grasp.

The hungry beast clamps his mouth tight to get a better grip. But the fish slips and splashes into the sea. Spinosaurus swipes his clawed hand through the water to grab the big fish. Then he flips it into the air and catches it in his toothy jaws.

He holds the struggling fish tightly in his jaws and turns towards the shore. There he spots Giganotosaurus.

Fossils show that some fish living at the same time as Spinosaurus grew up to 6 metres (20 feet) long. These fish would have made a decent meal for even the largest Spinosaurus.

FIERCE FACT

BIG MEAL

Giganotosaurus has been watching Spinosaurus splashing in the water. The giant meat-eater sees the huge fish hanging from Spinosaurus' mouth. He suddenly feels hungry.

Giganotosaurus stomps into the water and heads straight for Spinosaurus. He quickly reaches his opponent. He roars and thrusts his massive head forward. He snaps his jaws shut on the fish.

Spinosaurus tries to jerk the fish away, but Giganotosaurus holds on tightly. The two giant predators tug again. Suddenly, the fish breaks apart. Giganotosaurus stumbles deeper into the water. He's already lost his balance when a towering wave slams against him. He plunges into the dark sea.

Giganotosaurus means "giant southern lizard".

FIERCE FACT
NAME

Giganotosaurus crashes into the wet sand beneath the water. He lifts his head and climbs to his feet. But Spinosaurus is waiting for him. He snaps his long jaws around Giganotosaurus' neck.

Giganotosaurus roars. Spinosaurus holds on tight. He tugs his opponent further into the water. Giganotosaurus stumbles and falls to his knees. Spinosaurus forces his enemy's head below the dark waves. He leans his massive body weight against his foe to hold him under the water.

Giganotosaurus tries to roar. But his mouth fills with salty water. He begins to panic. He finds the sandy bottom with his feet and pushes up with all his strength. He rises wildly out of the foamy water. But Spinosaurus is still gripping his neck. The two giant dinosaurs topple sideways and crash into the stormy sea.

FIERCE FACT

NAME

Spinosaurus means
"spine lizard".

Giganotosaurus climbs to his feet first. Spinosaurus still clings to his enemy's neck. Giganotosaurus jerks his head back and forth. He flops like a fish trying to break free from Spinosaurus' grip. Dark blood seeps from Giganotosaurus' neck and streams into the water.

Spinosaurus finally finds his footing and tugs back on Giganotosaurus. Giganotosaurus roars and slashes at Spinosaurus with his clawed hand. But his arm is too short. His swing misses his huge opponent.

A giant wave suddenly crashes into the two monsters. Spinosaurus loses his footing, but he still hangs on to his enemy. Giganotosaurus charges out of the water and onto the beach, dragging Spinosaurus with him.

Spinosaurus' weight causes Giganotosaurus to stumble. He falls and crashes down on top of his enemy. Spinosaurus finally loses his grip on Giganotosaurus' neck. Both dinosaurs struggle to climb to their feet.

Spinosaurus rises first. He opens his jaws wide. He darts his head forward to strike. But Giganotosaurus ducks out of the way. He springs forward and clamps his powerful jaws on to Spinosaurus' neck. Spinosaurus shrieks and tries to pull away.

Giganotosaurus twists violently with his powerful neck muscles and massive body. There's a loud snap! Giganotosaurus lets go of Spinosaurus' neck. Spinosaurus flops to the ground. The battle is over.

Giganotosaurus stomps powerfully in the wet sand. He points his huge head towards the stormy sky and bellows a mighty roar. He lets the world know he's just beaten one of the biggest predators ever to walk the earth!

GLOSSARY

carnivore animal that eats only meat

extinct no longer living. An extinct animal is one whose kind has died out completely.

fossil remains or traces of plants and animals that are preserved as rock

herbivore animal that eats only plants

nostril opening in an animal's nose through which it breathes and smells

predator animal that hunts other animals for food

prey animal hunted by another animal for food

serrated having a jagged edge that helps with cutting, such as a saw

stocky having a strong, heavy build

FIND OUT MORE

BOOKS

Dinosaur Encyclopedia, Caroline Bingham
   (Dorling Kindersley, 2007)

Dinosaur Hunters: Palaeontologists, Louise and
   Richard Spilsbury (Heinemann Library, 2007)

Prehistoric Scary Creatures, John Malam
   (Book House, 2008)

WEBSITE

www.nhm.ac.uk/kids-only/dinosaurs
Visit the Natural History Museum's website to discover
more than 300 types of dinosaur, play dinosaur games,
and find out what sort of dinosaur you would be!

PLACES TO VISIT

Dinosaur Isle
Sandown, Isle of Wight PO36 8QA
www.dinosaurisle.com

Natural History Museum
London SW7 5BD
www.nhm.ac.uk

The Dinosaur Museum
Dorchester DT1 1EW
www.thedinosaurmuseum.com

INDEX

Argentinosaurus 17

extinction 7

Giganotosaurus
   attack style 17, 27, 28
   claws 15, 27
   food 10, 15, 17
   fossils 15
   head 22, 24, 28
   jaws 14, 22, 28
   name 23
   neck 24, 27, 28
   packs 17
   range 7
   size 7, 9, 28
   speed 10
   teeth 14

meat-eaters 4, 5, 7, 12, 13,
   16, 18, 22

plant-eaters 4, 17

Spinosaurus
   arms 13
   attack style 16, 24, 28
   claws 13, 20
   food 11, 12, 16, 21
   fossils 11, 12
   jaws 12, 20, 24, 28
   name 26
   neck 16, 20, 28
   range 7
   sail 8, 9
   size 7, 8, 9, 24, 28
   snout 16, 17, 20
   speed 11
   teeth 12, 16, 20

Tyrannosaurus rex 7